Acknowledgements

Sean Adams - for giving me insight and helping shape the title of the book, as well as helping me rethink the overall format and layout to make it more readable. To Richard White, who always believed I could write a book, but passed away before he could see this one. For my wife Eileen, who's always been supportive, no matter what I do. And most importantly, my thanks for God's amazing grace… who saved a wretch like me.

The Ultimate Church Marketing Guide
Know how to make smart advertising decisions

Table of Contents

- Why This Book?
- How To Use This Book
- What This Book Won't Do
- Your 'Farm' Market
- ABCs of Successful Retail Advertising
- Language
- How To Create A Great Logo Design
- Planning
- Digital
- Direct Mail
- Neighborhood Marketing
- Broadcast TV
- Cable
- Radio
- Other Media
- Other Observations About Advertising

WHY THIS BOOK

As a church leader, you're supposed to be a speechmaker, bookkeeper, business manager, counselor, and a whole lot more.

And now you need to be a marketing genius too?

That's why this book was written – to give you an overview of retail advertising and marketing principals (as they apply to the local level), so you can *know how to make smart advertising decisions.*

If you're like most pastors, you probably didn't get much (if any) formal education about marketing. Maybe you've picked up something along the way, through other pastors, resources or trial-and-error.

This book was written to help you.

As a marketer, I spent over 40 years helping local companies sell more product. Not on Madison Avenue, but in the trenches at the local level, helping small businesses market to their core service area – usually within a 2-5 mile radius.

I was one of the founding principals in what has become the nation's largest local advertising agency.

This book leverages my learned experience in local retail advertising and applies it to churches. Whether you realize it or not, your church is a RETAIL PRODUCT.

By RETAIL, we mean that you're 'selling' your message and product to the general public – not business-to-business.

And your church is a PRODUCT that has to be advertised and marketed to get new people in the door.

What Is Marketing?

One of my mentors, John Caraway, had this explanation: "Marketing is everything that gets a customer in the door, and keeps them coming back for more."

Following that definition, marketing includes your signage, your website, your social presence and a whole lot more. It's everything that people come in contact with – which together makes up your BRAND.

HOW TO USE THIS BOOK

The Ultimate Church Marketing Guide was written so that it could be read at different levels. At the highest level, it touches on a media and gives you a 40,000-foot overview. Maybe you never plan to use a particular marketing channel – you can just read the overview and skip the rest.

Maybe you're already familiar with the subject but want to know more. So, we've included more information for you to dive in deeper.

The Only Thing We Really Know... Is That We Don't Know.

Advertising can be tough. Sometimes when you do two mailings that are exactly the same, you get very different results. What works in Peoria may not work in Philadelphia. This is because advertising is part science and part art. There are a lot of variables (color, type, photos, headlines, copy, etc.) that go into an ad, and any of those elements could affect the outcome.

Here's how to make the best of every campaign:
1. *Use tested methods for creating your message.*
2. *Run your materials by a 3rd party to see what their reaction is.*
3. *Use your own common sense to review the piece.*
4. *Make sure you have a Call-To-Action, or you won't be able to gauge the response easily.*

Once your advertising has launched, do a group debrief with your staff. What was right? What could have been improved? What was missing? How did it compare to other similar advertising efforts? You may not be able to find the ultimate answers, but you will probably find some guidance to use in your next ad.

WHAT THIS BOOK WON'T DO

I'd like to make one thing clear about this book. This book is not about your 'product'. And by product, we're talking about your church and its DNA.

Where you're located, who you appeal to, the type of music you have and the messages you deliver, along with everything else makes up your 'product.' It's an integral part of your church's DNA.

The purpose of this book is not to discuss or change your product. As Popeye says: "I AM what I AM, and that's all that I AM."

This book will help you market what you "AM."

One note of caution. If you're in doubt about what you "AM", hold off your marketing until you're sure.

We're not talking about the normal evolution every church goes through as it changes service times, adds different types of services, or modifies the music. We're talking about making major changes to your church because you feel you are not really reaching your target market.

If you're reading this and feel uncomfortable about who you are as a church, put this book down, reshape your church, and come back when your new shape is underway.

Also, this book is not about internal communication or processes. There are hundreds of resources that can help you communicate with your regular attendees. The same goes for what happens once a person walks through the front door.

The focus of this book is to help you get new people (prospects) to your church for the first time.

YOUR 'FARM' MARKET

Real Estate agents like to refer to their home territory as their 'farm' market. While some business *could* come from across town, most of their business is conducted in a much smaller, more concentrated area.

The same is true for churches. While you could potentially draw from anywhere, your best market is usually closest to you.

How close? One adage I was told years ago was that a church's primary market was 5 Stoplights.

What does that mean? It means that if you put your church in the center of a map, and then head outward by 5 Stoplights in all directions, this is the distance that people are willing to travel to attend on a regular basis.

Examining this adage over the years, I've found it to be pretty accurate. If you're in a more rural area, 5 Stoplights takes you out farther, and people are used to traveling farther for everything.

In an urban setting, the 5 Stoplights are closer together.

Sometimes we'll refer to this area as your church's 'Footprint' or 'Target Market Area."

GETTING THE RIGHT LIST & THE RIGHT NAMES FOR DIRECT MAIL

If you're like most churches, you'll be using direct mail for some part of your marketing plan. Here's where understanding your 'Farm Market' comes into play.

According to the experts, a mailing list accounts for 40-60% of a campaign's success. In fact, it's possibly the most important element of a successful direct mail campaign.

Regardless of the message, if your mailer is sent to the right people it still has a decent chance of working. On the flipside, a great looking piece will have little chance of getting a response if it's sent to the wrong audience.

How do you find the right audience? Using your current member list, as described above, is a great place to start. Target the same neighborhoods for greatest success, because 'birds of a feather flock together.'

What does that mean? Millions have been spent in geo-demographic research to prove that people in the same neighborhoods tend to have the same habits. This applies to almost all lifestyle and buying characteristics.

A good mailing house can also take your current member list and extract demographics and lifestyle traits to create an overall 'Suspect' profile. Then that profile can be used in selecting lists and making smart advertising decisions.

<u>Map It Out</u>

Try the 5 Stoplights for yourself and see if it's true for your church. Get a map and mount it on foam core and circle the stoplights. (Or do it digitally.)

Next, take a list of your members and regular attendees and put a pin in for each family.

This takes a little time, but the process is key to understanding who you're reaching and who you're not.

You'll see a few people who fall outside the 5 Stoplights zone. Sometimes these are older members who have moved but still attend. There will be a few others that are outside as well, and it's not important as to why.

What you're after is to create a map of where your core audience (80%) is coming from. This will also help tell you where to target for growth.

<u>An Avatar Is A Great Way to Visualize Your Best Customer</u>

In his book "The Secrets of Business Mastery", Mike Agugliaro talks about building a customer Avatar.

He says your customer avatar should be a representation or an icon or an ideal – a single thing that reminds you of all others like it. Your avatar would be your ideal member or prospect - a very detailed word-picture of exactly the kind of member you want to serve.

Mike says that you can't get too detailed in this exercise. The more detailed you can get, the closer you'll be to defining the people who will come to visit and have the greatest potential to stay as members.

Use some of these characteristics:
- *What do they look like?*
- *How old are they?*
- *Where do they live?*
- *What kind of home do they live in?*
- *How old is their home?*
- *Do they have kids?*
- *How old are their kids?*
- *Do they like to pay with credit? Cash?*
- *Where do they shop?*
- *What's their favorite color?*
- *What kind of car do they drive?*
- *What kind of job do they have?*
- *How much money do they make?*
- *Where do they hang out?*

The list can go on and on. The more detailed you make it, the easier it will be to find your perfect customer, and then to create marketing that connects directly with them.

Note: It's possible that if you're located in a diverse market that you'll have multiple target customers.

Creating marketing becomes simpler after you have built your perfect customer avatar. To connect with your audience, you'll be speaking to them in a way that they understand and demonstrates your awareness of the things that are important to them. Your marketing can do a better job of how your church can serve them and help solve their problems

If you're wondering if creating marketing that only one type of customer would find compelling, pushes away other prospective customers, the answer is that it does. And while your church is welcoming to all, you want your marketing to have a focus – a focus on the very best type of prospect.

Here's how Mike recommends you take action:
__ Think about your ideal member. Consider the members that made you say, "I wish all my members were like that one!" Write down the qualities and characteristics of this ideal member. Be as detailed as possible. By the end, you should have a very clear description of who this member is and what they are like.
__ Start creating marketing messages for this ideal member by focusing in on the benefits that they will gain by attending.
__ Review other marketing to help you to get into their head, even if it's totally unrelated. Understand what else they are buying and doing, and why they are doing it.

Add your own actions:
__ Stop doing actions (Actions you currently do now but should stop doing)
__ Keep doing actions (Actions you currently do now and should keep doing)
__ Start doing actions (Actions you don't do now but should start doing)
__ Who will do new actions? (Assign the action to yourself or someone else)
__ By when? (When will these actions be complete?)

A.B.C.S OF SUCCESSFUL RETAIL ADVERTISING

Here's the secret to great retail advertising, which we call the A. B. C.s to help remember the principals.

<u>A</u> = Arresting Visual.
This is the stopping power. Does your piece, whether it's a direct mailer or a television commercial, grab someone's attention and keep them from throwing it away or ignoring it? Maybe you'll use a bright color, a dramatic visual or photography of people. Or a combination.

<u>B</u> = Benefit Headline.
Communicates "What's In It for Me."
At heart, we're all selfish, so it's always about putting the right benefits (not features) in front of the customer.
Example: "Your children will *love* our Kid's Program. (And you will too!)"

<u>C</u> = Call To Action.
Give me a reason to act on this *now*. Why should I do this today? What incentive are you going to give me to not wait?

While this concept works very well for virtually every retailer in America, it's usually foreign to churches.

<u>A simple Response Device can boost attendance and give you a key added benefit.</u>

The Response Device is a very common advertising principal that you encounter every day. FREE UMBRELLA WITH CADILLAC TEST DRIVE. FREE DESSERT ON WEDNESDAY NIGHTS.

"But giving something away for attendance? Are you crazy?"

Maybe a little crazy. But we can tell you that it works because consumers are conditioned by the hundreds of offers that constantly bombard them. Why not leverage it?

You could try a free gift, like a Bible, or a pamphlet on a popular topic that could tie to the current sermon series. "7 Steps to Help Get Your Children Under Control." Some churches have used $5 Subway Gift Cards very successfully.

Ideally, the offer should be valuable enough that they're instantly motivated to respond. "What would get you off the couch and into a church?"

Give yourself the best chance to succeed by putting the best possible offer on the table. If you're sending out a meager offer, don't be surprised with a meager response.

The key benefit of the RESPONSE DEVICE is tracking. If you include this offer in your next mailing, it will give you a better idea of how the mailing worked. It will help you gauge the response in general terms – Was it great, average, or poor?

Yes, you will have to think through the details of the offer: Expiration Date, Qualifiers (new attendees only?), Must Present Mailer/Coupon, etc.

Another way to create response is to go in a different direction by using a start date. "New series starts this weekend." But don't make the date more than one week in advance – families just don't plan that far ahead in today's world.

If you're in doubt about how offers work, consider these offers I received in my email box:

> Purchase a Penthouse at Trump Residences Toronto and get a Steinway Piano Player for a month, on us. (A purchase of the 5501 Penthouse comes with the Steinway Grand Piano signed by world-famous musician, Lang Lang.)
>
> -and-
>
> Receive a Rolls-Royce car with every purchase of a Penthouse at Trump Residences Toronto.

All these properties are in the millions, but it proves that even the super-rich respond to the right offer!

LANGUAGE

Regardless of whether your church is conservative or progressive, it pays to comb your copy for certain words that today's audience just doesn't understand or has a negative connotation to them.

When you're advertising, you're trying to communicate to non-attendees so shift gears and look for words that might confuse them.

Too often, these keywords are used internally out of habit. Consider modifying them when you're using them in your advertising and marketing.

Instead of:	Consider:
Sermon	Message
Denomination	(Just use your domination or affiliation instead)
Gospel	The first 4 books of the New Testament in the Bible - or - Bible chapters Mathew, Mark, Luke & John – or – The Good News
Litany	Prayer
Liturgy	Worship
Parishioner	Member
Hymn	Song
Ecclesiastic	Church
Messiah	Jesus

Just do a quick review of your ad before finalizing them. Have you used any words that your prospective attendee might not understand?

Using People In Your Advertising.

Should you use people in your advertising? We think the answer is Yes, Yes and Yes. It works because people can relate to other people – having fun, enjoying themselves, getting a great message, and watching their children being properly cared for.
Here are some tips on using people:
1. *Try to use shots that are close enough/tight enough that you can see the emotion on the person's face. A crowd shot typically doesn't work, unless there's someone in the foreground.*

2. *Make sure the shot is of high quality. If you have a member or staff that can take great pictures, go for it! Just make sure to get signed model releases for anyone's face that's identifiable. (Find a sample Model Release in the Reference Section.)*
3. *There's nothing wrong with using stock photography. In fact, it's probably your best and easiest source for many of shots you need. Sources like IStock, ShutterStock, and ThinksStock have thousands of affordable shots. Plus, there are lots of other sources with free stock photography.*
4. *You'll reap what you sow. If you want to attract children, make sure to show pictures of them. The same goes for youths, elderly, diversity, etc. You're more likely to get more of the same type of people that you feature in your advertising.*

HOW TO CREATE A GREAT LOGO DESIGN

Having an attractive and effective logo design is very important to your church. It's one of the first things a customer sees, and it connects all your collateral pieces together. Your logo is your representative to the community and the core element of your brand identity.

You're more likely to stick with a logo for the long-term if you take the time investing in a design you really love. The longer you stick with a logo, the stronger the brand awareness for your church. This doesn't mean that your logo can't evolve with the times, and great logos usually do.

How do you come up with a great logo design that will give you the impact and communication you're looking for? According to Milton Glaser, designer of the world famous "I Love New York" logo, simplicity is key.

Here are four things he recommends for a great logo design:

Make It Unique
Whether we like to admit it, there's usually a lot of competition in the marketplace. That's why your logo needs to be unique and stand out in the crowd. You want prospects to see your logo design and immediately think of you, not other churches. One way is to avoid using common symbols and phrases. (The Cross is the most commonly used logo symbol.) Your logo doesn't have to literally show what your business does. Instead, think outside of the box. Designer David Airy points to some great examples, "The Mercedes logo isn't a car. The Virgin Atlantic logo isn't an airplane. The Apple logo isn't a computer."

Make It Adaptable
If your logo design is simple, then it will adapt to all situations very easily. When creating a logo, it helps to remember the phrase "K.I.S.S. Keep It Simple Silly." What message will your logo convey on a business card versus a billboard? In a perfect world, your logo will have the same effect on potential customers no matter how or where you use it. Think about the size and color of the logo. It's best if you start with a black and white version because eventually your logo will be used that way at some point in time. Some elements that look good in 4 color or multi-color don't always translate as

colors are removed. Shading and drop shadows don't always work when reduced, so look at your logo small (1/2") and large so you can see the logo from different perspectives.

Make It Appropriate
Choosing colors carefully for your design is vital, according to professional Matt Mickiewicz. "Different colors are associated with different meanings in different cultures. It's important to think about how the colors in your logo reflect your brand values and the services or products you sell." While your logo design doesn't have to show what you do specifically, it should be appropriate for your customers. This goes for both color and styling. If you owned a children's boutique, for example, your style and colors could be bright and whimsical. But they wouldn't be appropriate for an accountant.

Make It Timeless
Marilyn Monroe once said that "True beauty is timeless." The same holds true for great logo designs. Logos that have been around for decades are easily recognizable among consumers, even as the brands have evolved. Clean lines, symmetry, and neutrality all contribute to making a timeless design – one that can stand the test of time.

PLANNING

How do you plan and budget?

One of the ways is to start with a budget. Most retail businesses of similar sizes budget between 5% and 10% of their total revenues for advertising and marketing. James Dalman, a church marketing authority, says that established churches should consider allocating 10%-15% of their overall church budget per year for marketing and communications. O.K., so we know you're in the right ballpark with 5% to 15%. Most churches include internal communication in this percentage, for things like a web site, logo, worship slides, video clips, visitor's packet, etc.

The truth is that you'll never have enough, but the more you spend, the more you'll grow. Why? Because you're working with the typical sales & marketing funnel as it applies to churches.

Church Marketing Funnel

Suspects:	Anyone within your Target Area/"Farm Market". Households usually define this. Get Total Suspects by multiplying Households by 2.54
Prospects:	These are people who you've had some type of contact with. They used to be a Suspect, but once you've 'touched' them in some way, they've become a Prospect. Maybe they know someone who attends. For simplicity's sake, let's say you've targeted 4 key neighborhoods, and have mailed to those households 3 times last year. That's your total number of prospects.
Attendees:	This is your total attendance for all services for a defined period. This assumes you're doing a head count at each service. This includes all new visitors.
Members:	This is people who have joined your church, but it could also be regular attendees – those who you have an address, email or other contact info. Your Members/Regular Attendees number is important because you'll subtract it for your overall attendance to find out how many new people you're attracting.

Note that this isn't a perfect science, and there are a lot of areas that can 'slip'. But if you do this week after week, you will be able to better gauge how marketing efforts are working.

Let's look at a sample funnel.

25,400 Suspects	There are 10,000 Households in your Target Area/"Farm Market" x 2.54 people per household = 25,400
2,540 Prospects	You mailed to your 4 target neighborhoods with 1,000 total homes. 1,000 homes x 2.54 people per household = 2,540 prospects.
550 Attendees	This was your total weekly attendance.
500 Members	Including regular attendees.

If we take Attendees (550) and subtract Members (500), we have 50 new visitors that attended. If there was no other outside influence, we can assume that your mailing brought in the 50 new people.

Here's what's challenging. Sometimes you'll do a mailing (or other marketing push) and your numbers will go down! That's because your overall attendance may be down for any number of reasons. Maybe the weather's bad. Or maybe the weather's good. Or maybe your city's team is in the playoffs. That's why you need to track the attendance every week if you're not already doing it.

It also helps to include a Response Device in your advertising.

The Center for Church Communications says that 76% of churches aren't documenting or tracking the results of their marketing. Don't be one of the 76% - be one of the 24% who's marketing smarter.

You'll also need to calculate your conversions. Each church is very different, so these numbers are highly individualized. Of the prospects who attend (visitors), how many ultimately turn into members/regular attendees? This will help you chart a path to your overall church growth. Don't forget to subtract the percentage of people that you lose, for whatever reason.

<u>Newly Planted?</u>

If you're a newly planted church, the percentage method for budgeting won't really work, because you don't have the base income to work from.

Budget as much as you possibly can. Some church leaders like to think of their marketing budget as a mission investment and not an expense. In reality, it's both.

With smaller budgets, it's even more important that each piece work as hard as it can. But you also want to avoid using something where you didn't spend enough that the medium works. An example could be a single mailing to a household, whereas at least 3 mailings are needed to get a response.

What's your average attendee worth?

Another perspective on budgeting is to look at what marketers call the Lifetime Value of a Customer. In this case, it would be the lifetime value of that attendee.

Does putting a value on a member offend you? Don't let it. After all, you're a business with income and expenses like any other.

According to Stephen Anderson, author of "Before You Build", the average giving amount per person is $1,038. Multiply this amount by the average number of years people attend your church. Let's use 5 years as an example. (Adjust these numbers as needed for your individual circumstances.)

$1,038 x 5 (years) = $5,190 Lifetime Value of each Customer (attendee).

<u>Return On Investment</u>

If your conversion rate (how many new attendees become regular attendees) is 20%, then you can calculate your return on the money you 'invested' in a marketing activity.

Here's an example.

Let's say you did a mailing to 10,000 households and your total cost was $3,000. Of the 10,000 mailed, 1% visited. (10,000 x .01 = 100)
100 Visitors x 20% conversion rate = 20 Regular attendees
20 Regular Attendees x $1,038 per year = $20,760 (or $103,800 over 5 years)

You'll need to plug in your own church's numbers, but the formulas work the same.

YEAR-LONG OR SEASONAL PLANNING?

One perspective is to look at your marketing in two distinct strategies: YEAR-LONG PROGRAMS AND SEASONAL INITIATIVES.

YEAR-LONG PROGRAMS: These strategies are designed to encourage a steady stream of new attendees throughout the year. As an example, maintaining an SEO-optimized website and social media presence both are year-long programs that will drive new attendees regardless of the season. So is doing small mailings every week, for follow-up or to homes near new members.

SEASONAL INITIATIVES: Because the church business is cyclical, with two big events every year, the role of seasonal marketing initiatives is crucial. Increasing your marketing before Easter and Christmas will certainly increase your attendance on these key holidays.

But what about other key times that are important, but secondary. For some churches, that's when children go back to school in the fall. Or right after the first of the year, when resolutions are made. What is your experience in your market?

Conversely, don't turn off the tap completely if you're moving into a known slower time. If you have a year-round strategy in place, that may be enough to cover you. Or you may need to lower expectations about your results. Maybe a direct mailer only pulls 50% as well in the doldrums of summer, usually a slow time for most churches. What's important is that it still pulled new attendees.

DIGITAL

This chapter of the book is the shortest, but also the most important.

Why is it the most important? Because digital marketing (PPC, SEO, Social, Website, Email) will be your most effective (and cost-effective) channels of advertising. All trends are toward making this more true than less true.

Why is this chapter the shortest? Because there are hundreds of resources for you to access, especially with rapidly changing ad channels. Rather than try to "rewrite the book", (which would be out-of-date upon publishing), we'd rather give you 10 Keys to Digital Advertising Success.

1. Have A Point Person
   You'll need someone who understands the key aspects of digital marketing. They don't have to be a programmer or a PPC specialist, but they should understand how all the components work. Maybe they're a member of the congregation, or you hire someone to work part-time.

2. Prioritize
   Understand that you don't have to do all things digital to be successful. Make a list of each element in priority order and attack them as you have resources (financial and people) available.

3. Do each element well, or not at all.
   For example, if having a good website is at the top of your list, make sure it works – no broken links, current pictures, it's mobile-friendly, etc. - all the basic blocking and tackling elements that give a visitor confidence that you're the 'real deal." Does your website need to have the latest bells and whistles? No, it doesn't. But it should do a good job of representing your 'DNA' and what you're about. If you have a CONTACT US on your website, do you have a process in place to respond within XX hours?

4. Website first. All other things to follow.
   We believe that your website should be your first priority for digital assets and marketing. In most cases, it will be the hub toward which everything is directed. Don't have the resources to add a content-rich Facebook

page? That's o.k. as long as you have a good website. Same goes for an outbound email campaign.

5. Talent is closer than you think.
Among your members/regular attenders, you'll more than likely have people with skills in digital marketing. Maybe they don't even realize it. You've probably got several members who are really adept at Facebook and use it daily. Given the right supervision (your Point Person) and guidelines, they can help create a robust and content rich Facebook page at little or no cost. Service toward digital efforts is just as important and relevant as your Parking Team, Counting Team or Greeters. Just like those teams, you'll need to recruit, establish guidelines and divide responsibilities so that no one is overwhelmed.

6. Micromanaging will kill any digital initiative.
If you put the right people in place, guided by your Point Person, and you establish guidelines, each digital effort should be able to run effectively on its own. But if you insist that every Facebook posting be pre-approved by 6 people, including yourself, you'll cripple the efforts. Should you be concerned about what's posted? Of course. But it's easy enough to craft a Facebook Posting Guidelines for team members to use. If they come across something that's not covered in the guidelines, then they know to stop, check with the Point Person, who resolves it or escalates it as needed.

7. Have a proofing process in place.
A misspelled word reflects badly on your whole organization. It can put visitors into a spin: "If they don't take care of this detail, what about my details? Will they lose my email address? Will they get my prayer request wrong?" It's not rational, but it occurs with more frequency than you can imagine. The solution is simple. Put a process in place to proof materials before they are published or sent out. Obviously, this applies to all marketing materials, not just digital ones.

8. Once you have your website (and Facebook) in place, focus on your existing base.
You've probably heard that it requires a lot less money and effort to keep current customers in a business, rather than seeking new ones. The same

strategy applies to your overall digital strategy. Make sure you're communicating well with your visitors and regular attendees before spending money to get new ones. An example: If you have the choice of spending resources on improving your follow-up emails, or spending it on PPC, we'd suggest the email efforts. You might look at these as Internal Efforts vs. External Efforts.

9. A good digital strategy is multi-faceted and interactive.
   Each digital element is connected with others by the simple click of a mouse. Ultimately, your digital solution will have many parts; all interacting together. Don't expect one 'silver bullet' to solve everything. This doesn't mean that you have to be doing everything digitally to be successful either. As was mentioned above, do each element well, and add more as resources allow.

10. People resources are more important than financial ones.
    It's easy to create a new digital initiative that is affordable financially because many things digital are people-driven rather than money-driven. But always make sure you have the people resources to manage the effort. If you don't, you'll have a new program that doesn't work as effectively as it should, or worse, it could reflect badly on your overall image.

DIRECT MAIL

Direct mail is usually a core marketing vehicle for churches because of the ability to target a particular area. Even though the cost to reach 1,000 people (CPM-Cost Per Thousand) can be higher than other media, there is usually very little waste if done correctly. So, your net cost is very good.

Direct mail postcards can be the most inexpensive, effective, and targeted marketing strategy available to you today. Because if planned correctly, you can have very little, if any, waste. You can deliver a full-color, personalized marketing message to a suspect's front door very cost-efficiently. And unlike e-mail, postcards are not subject to "DELETE" or
"BLOCK SENDER" keys with a simple click of the mouse.

But is direct mail dead?

There's no doubt that digital marketing channels like social, email, mobile and digital display have changed the game, especially in the last few years.

But with every challenge, there's always an opportunity. Many marketers are aggressively using direct mail to cut through the clutter and deliver unique, one-to-one communications to current and potential customers.

Here's one of the reasons why. 70% of Americans believe that direct mail is more personal than digital communications, according to a survey done by the provider Compu-Mail.

"Direct mail as a marketing media continues to deliver strong results for marketers. In fact, in many categories of business, it is the primary lead generation tool," says Wes Sparling, VP of marketing strategy at IWCO Direct.

Contrary to what many people may think, direct mail is experiencing growth with a domestic gross spend of $44.5 billion (in 2014), according to Winterberry Group. The U.S. Postal Service reports that standard mail volume increased by 3% within the last 9-month period.

"Direct mail has a long, proven history as a successful advertising medium. Just because there is a new advertising option available, it doesn't mean that it will work better than direct mail," says Craig Simpson, mail consultant and author of the Direct Mail Solution: A Business Owner's Guide to Building a Lead-Generating, Sales-Driving, Money-Making Direct-Mail Campaign.

Sparling of IWCO Direct says that digital is not a direct mailer's foe, but instead gives marketers access to one of the industry's most powerful tools: data. "When using segmentation, data, analytics, and appropriate format and messaging, direct mail is unquestionably one of the best media available for customer acquisition," Sparling says. He notes "By looking at the whole mix of marketing media and assessing each of them for their relative strengths and weaknesses... a marketer can develop an optimal acquisition strategy."

Sparling says that while a person's age should be considered, the assumption that direct mail campaigns work better on older audiences isn't always true. "A smart marketer is able to identify which tactics best reach his or her target audience and then through testing and measurement will allocate their marketing dollars toward a mix of tactics that best benefits the campaign's objectives."

Some experts say that direct mail is not out of date but is simply too pricey for some marketing budgets. That's why they're turning to more co-mingled or shared mail. This category of direct marketing has grown more rapidly in the last few years.

According to Simpson, marketers need to take a closer look at direct mail as it continues to be a strong performer in customer acquisition. "I see results from direct mail campaigns every week, and I can tell you it is alive and well," Simpson says. "Direct mail continues to provide a consistent response for generating new customers and getting existing customers to buy more often. There is less competition in the mailbox, so you have a better chance of getting noticed by your prospects and customers."

There are many different types of mail options, but here are some you're most likely to use.

NON-PROFIT RATE

The US Postal Service has a special postage rate for churches, which allows you to pay just 7.9 cents per piece. For large mailings, the savings can really add up.

You do this through a nonprofit mailing permit that costs $180 to apply, and then another $180 for the yearly permit.

If that's too large an amount for you to be comfortable, you can through another organization that already has the permit and skip the fees. These are called cooperative mailings, and they're specifically allowed in the USPS guidelines.

Both of the organizations must be authorized to send mail at the special rate—but only one needs to have the permit. That means your church could soon be sending mail to members, guests, and others at the reduced rate - with no extra expense.

Many mailing companies that specialize in church mailings can help you. They can drop ship to any post office and send your mail at nonprofit rates using their non-profit permit. This is called ghost permitting, also known as "request to mail at a post office other than your own."

EVERY DOOR DIRECT

Every Door Direct Mail is a service available from the United States Postal Service (USPS). Many people also refer to it as Saturation Mail.

With very low rates, it can be a cost-effective way to reach potential attendees. It can be self-service - use the USPS online tool to select postal routes and pay for postage online. Next, bring your mailing to your local Post Office for delivery to every household on your chosen routes.

Many people assume that saturation mailing uses ZIP Codes, when in fact the actual definitions from the USPS for the maximum saturation discount use the carrier route as the defining region.

One extra plus with Every Door Direct is there's no need to buy addresses or mailing lists. (You can make the decision to exclude businesses.) The downside is that you have 'buy' 90%+ of the residential homes within a Carrier Route.

The USPS offers special rates available for churches and other nonprofit organizations that are considerably lower than regular rates, but not everyone can qualify. Just because you were granted nonprofit status from the IRS does NOT mean you have been granted nonprofit mailing status from the US Postal System. You must apply for this status.

You also need to make sure that the material being mailed complies with strict requirements for nonprofit rates.

The current saturation price for nonprofit organizations is about 7 cents per piece.

<u>What's A Carrier Route?</u>

It's a group of addresses to which the USPS assigns the same code to aid in mail delivery. Typically, each carrier route is related to where a particular mail carrier delivers.

ZIP+4 codes are not the same as a carrier routes. Each carrier route can contain tens or hundreds of ZIP+4 codes.

FIRST CLASS MAIL

When you mail First-Class, no special preparation is required before mailing. You just need to make sure of your addresses are correct for timely and consistent processing and delivery of your postcards. You can mail 1 piece or 100. Using First Class mail is a great way to send follow-ups to those new attendees. Or any other type of personalized message. Whether it's hand-written or just hand addressed, you'll probably use First Class for your low volume mail.

There is a lower rate for smaller postcards that are at least 3 1/2 inches high, 5 inches long, and .007-inch-thick, but no more than 4 1/4 inches high, 6 inches long. You can use a doubled card (like a reply card) too, if you follow the USPS guidelines.

PRESORTED FIRST-CLASS

If you're mailing at least 500 addressed pieces at a time, you can qualify for Presorted First-Class mail discounts.
You must also follow some additional steps to qualify. Each piece must be marked "Presorted" or "PRSRT" and "First-Class", letter trays must be used, pieces need to be banded when presorted and trayed, etc.

You'll also have to pay an annual $150.00 presort mailing fee and use a certified process at least once a year to ensure the accuracy of 5-digit ZIP codes.

Usually, this discount is best achieved through your printer or mailing house that can handle the details and requirements. They can also help you with other available discounts that you could qualify for.

SHARED MAIL

What Is Shared Mail? It's another low-cost way to reach thousands of prospects. It's typically a large double-sided, full-color sheet that is delivered with other mail in a shared mail program. Because it piggybacks or "shares" the delivery cost with other mail pieces, the cost per piece can be significantly lower than a standard postcard.

USPS delivers a Shared Mail 'bundle' in all mailboxes along the targeted carrier route, typically with weekly frequency. While USPS delivers Shared mail, you have to contract with a separate company to be included.

Valassis is the leading company in the U.S. for Shared Mail, but there are others. Many times, the daily newspaper offers a similar service.

Shared Mail is usually priced to be turn-key, included printing, distribution and even creative. Minimum quantities usually start at 20,000, but each company is different.

One footnote. If you're located in a smaller, more rural community, Shared Mail may not be available. It is typically only offered in denser metropolitan areas.

<u>It Pays To Hire Outside Help.</u>

Direct mail, especially when doing large mailings, is a complicated business, with technology having a major hand.

That's why we recommend finding a reputable firm to help you.

Most of the time, this will be a printer who has a comprehensive direct mail component, or conversely a direct mail company that has in-house printing.

They can help you in several ways, like running your address files through an address standardization process known as "CASS," following strict USPS guidelines. CASS checks the addresses against a USPS file of deliverable addresses, corrects any typos in your address file, and appends the ZIP+4 and carrier route codes.

Because of technology and associated discounts, a good direct mail house can deliver your mail at or below the same cost you could do it directly. They can also help you qualify for additional volume discounts.

A good direct mail house can take all the guesswork out of your mailings and make sure your mail is compliant with the USPS standards, especially for non-profit mailers.

They can also help you with targeting and demographic information.

Because they're an outside resource, it's like hiring an additional person on staff — but without the fixed cost or benefits.

There are also a number of secular direct mail companies that specialize in church mailings.

<u>90 Seconds, Or Less.</u>

If you do everything right when marketing with postcards, your prospect will decide to act in 90 seconds, or less. Here's what typically happens when a suspect gets your postcard in the mail:

Step 1: Suspect glances at postcard's image (billboard) side (3 seconds)
Step 2: Suspect then turns over to read return address side (5 seconds)
Step 3: Suspect reads headline (7 seconds)
Step 4: Suspect reads body copy (60 seconds)
Step 5: Suspect acts if message is interesting (15 seconds)

This typical path is why we stress the A.B.C.s of advertising.

For a definition of "Suspect' vs. "Prospect, see earlier description

<u>Checklist For Success</u>

Make sure your direct mail campaign has a plan. Here's a checklist of some of the key things needed to have the greatest success:

1. <u>What Do You Want To Accomplish</u>? XX number of new attendees?

2. <u>What Is a Customer Worth</u>? Covered earlier, you should know what you're willing to pay for a new attendee.

3. <u>What Is Your Budget</u>? How many new attendees do you need, and how much you will invest on a monthly or quarterly basis to keep generating a steady stream.

4. <u>Who Are You Targeting</u>? Who are your best 'Suspects'? What is their age, income, family type & size, and other psychological information?

5. <u>How Will You Follow Up</u>? Do you have a process in place for your church?

6. <u>How Will You Track the Results</u>? If you don't track the results, there is no way to know how your campaigns are working.

7. <u>What Basis Will You Use To Determine Success</u>? What's your benchmark, as it can vary church to church?

8. *What Is Your Offer?* Did you include something that has "get them off the couch" appeal?

9. *What Format Will You Use?* Letter? Small postcard? Large postcard?

10. *How Will You Communicate the Program To Your Staff?* Very important, but usually overlooked. Communicate all aspects of the campaign to anyone who might interface with incoming prospects.

11. *What Is the Time Frame?* You can't start planning too soon. Start your planning now.

HOW TO HELP MAKE SURE YOUR POSTCARD DOESN'T GET TRASHED.
Don't make this your direct mail nightmare. An ideal prospect receives the postcard you've spent a lot of time and money designing, printing and mailing … and they toss it right in the trash!

Yikes!

When you're marketing, you always want to avoid throwing your money away. And while a little waste happens in any direct mail campaign, you want to avoid it if possible and make sure your postcard is a lead-generating machine.

Let's assume that you've selected the right mailing list.

Now let's focus on attention. You have mere seconds to get the prospect's attention. Even if they don't act right away but you've gotten their attention, an impression is made.

There are three key factors for getting the most attention in direct mail.

1. Make sure you're using the right sized postcard.

Size plays a more important role for one very simple reason — the larger the card, the easier it is to see!

How do you find the perfect postcard size? Ask yourself these questions.

How frequently do other businesses (not just churches) in our area market themselves?

(If you live in the target area, lay out your daily mail 'package and take a snapshot of it. After doing this for 30 days, you'll have a really good idea of what you're up against.)

Your 'competition' isn't always other churches, but all other mail that arrives in your prospect's mailbox. If there's not a lot of mail that arrives daily, then you can probably go with a smaller card. But if the mailbox brings moderate to heavy amounts of mail, you definitely need a larger card.

If your offer is easy to understand, then you can consider a smaller card.

Don't let the cost of a larger postcard keep you from mailing a postcard that works. If it doesn't work, then you've spent even more money. Water doesn't boil at 211° - you have to get to 212°!

2. Is your postcard's headline clear?

You can't afford it to be confusing or uninteresting.

You have one shot with your headline to get the prospect's attention. That's why an an effective headline should clearly and concisely explain to the recipient how your church can improve their life/solve a problem/make their life easier in a way that is immediately clear.

If you have a unique selling proposition or a tagline, you can incorporate it into your headline, or even use it as your headline.

Here are some examples of church taglines that could be also used as postcard headlines:

- End Your Search for a Friendly, Spiritual Church
- Passionately helping people find & follow Jesus.
- Where people gather…to worship, share and learn.

- Building people through a loving, caring fellowship: Building a church through loving, caring people.
- Where Truth and Love Make a difference
- We Build Hope
- Large enough to serve you - Small enough to know you
- Transforming Lives and Building Dreams
- A Place For You
- Living Hope For Real People
- Proclaiming & Demonstrating the Love of God through Christ
- A Community Dedicated to Seeking God and Serving People
- A Church involved in & Caring About the Community
- Experience God's Presence – The Church That Cares
- Start a New Way of Living!
- Building Holy and Healthy Lives
- Growing Together
- Where God's Word & Spirit bring Freedom

Consider the classic sales mantra: W.I.I.F.M. – What's In It For Me? Does your headline pay off the benefits for the prospect?

3. Make sure that the images on your postcard reinforce your message

If the image on your postcard doesn't make your headline clearer, then it really isn't a good image to use. When it supports your headline, the force of your message is multiplied.

You want to make sure that your image grabs (and keeps) even more attention, so that prospects immediately understand exactly what's in it for them, following the W.I.I.F.M. example above.

<u>*Postcard Mania's 10 Important Elements To Make Sure Your Postcards Work.*</u>

Postcard Mania mails over 4 million postcards a week for over 69,000 customers. So, they know a thing or two about what works and what doesn't. They've developed this list of 10 things that are essential to success.
1. *Clear Bold Headline*
2. *The Offer*

3. *Contact Info*
4. *Call-To-Action*
5. *Logo*
6. *Subhead That Leads To Text*
7. *Benefits, Benefits, Benefits*
8. *Colors That Pop*
9. *Supporting Imagery*
10. *Return Address*

NEIGHBORHOOD MARKETING

Wouldn't it be cool to mail and invite to the homes around where your members lived, or around where a new prospect lives?

The concept works because people living in the same neighborhood are a lot alike. The reasons to attend a church like yours are usually similar too.

Logistically, this can be a challenge to get the lists and do regular mailings. It can be difficult and expensive to do in small quantities.

One company has changed that with a program they call RADIUS MARKETING from SmartleadsUSA.

Used primarily in the services business, it can work for your church as well, because micro-targeting your marketing around recent visits or members is a great idea.

Here's how it works.
1. You create a postcard design that leverages the 'neighbor' concept. i.e. "You'll never believe what your neighbor's done now!"
2. Go to SmartleadsUSA easy-to-use online interface and log in, enter a single address and submit your order.
3. You can send as few as 50 postcards per address.
4. You can upload multiple creative designs, and SmartleadsUSA can help you with the creative.
5. All are mailed using an oversized 11" x 6" postcard, printed using high-quality 4-color printing.

There simply isn't a lower cost, more effective program than SmartleadsUSA's RADIUS MARKETING. If you don't do any other external marketing activity, you should implement it.

http://www.smartleadsusa.com/radius/
888-795-6245
3535 Alternate 19
Palm Harbor, FL 34683

BROADCAST TELEVISION

Broadcast Television is one of the most powerful advertising vehicles. It has been since it's invention in the 1940s.

The combination of sight and sound has sold billions of dollars of products and services. And it may be able to help you too.

First, let's understand what Broadcast Television is. It's confusing because for most people, Broadcast TV is delivered via their cable system but that doesn't make it cable.

Broadcast TV is the 4-6 'local' channels, which are network affiliates: ABC, CBS, NBC and Fox, and sometimes CW. Typically they have local news and features. They also broadcast their network affiliate shows, usually in prime time. Other times of the day are usually filled with local and syndicated programming.

They sell advertising locally, within the broadcast area, which is called the DMA (Designated Market Area as defined by Nielsen).

Here's what important to you.

After you've done your plot of your market area, now you can go back and look to see how closely your target area fits with your market's DMA. (DMA maps can be obtained online or through any local TV rep.)

Unless you're in a smaller market or have a large church (or satellites), Broadcast TV will usually have too much waste. For example, the Tampa DMA covers 10 counties, and is approximately 130 miles tall (from Inverness down to Sarasota) and is 115 miles wide! (Including Sebring, FL.)

Even if you discount some of the less populated counties in the Tampa DMA, very few churches have that broad of a footprint.

When your footprint and media maps don't closely align, you have waste. You'll have some waste with any mass media, but you want to minimize it whenever possible.

What's A DMA?

A Designated Market Area (or DMA) is a geographic area that represents specific television markets as defined by and updated annually by the Nielsen Company. There are 210 DMA markets in the U.S. They are determined by the number of television households contained within that area and the percentage of that area's population in relation to the total U.S. population. Broadcast media planners often use traffic metrics from a certain DMA to determine how well a campaign performs. A DMA is different than an MSA, which is a definition used for radio.

<u>*When Is Waste Ever Acceptable?*</u>

Waste can be o.k. if your cost after calculating waste out is low enough. Cable TV, covered in another chapter, is typically twice as expensive as Broadcast TV. But it can be highly targeted to reduce waste. To calculate your real costs or 'after-waste' costs, here's the formula.

EXAMPLE:
Station WABC
- *Average Spot Cost: $100.00*
- *Average Reach: 5,000 (based on ADULTS 18+)*
- *Cost-Per-Thousand (CPM): $100. divided by 5 (,000) = $20 CPM*
- *Adjusted CPM, with 50% waste: $40*

Use the DMA map to compare it to your church's footprint. Is the DMA 3 times as big as your Target Market Area/Footprint? Then you'll have 33% waste. Twice as big? 50% waste.

CABLE TELEVISION

Cable television was originally invented in the late '40s to provide signals to homes in more rural areas that had a difficult time receiving Broadcast television. That's where it remained until the 1980s when cable companies began rapid expansion into all metropolitan areas.

Today, cable is a fixture in most households, and most delivery is digital. Hybrid fiber-coaxial cable (also called fiber-optic), from companies like Verizon's FiOS, expands the ability to deliver even more channels into the home.

Most cable systems are broken up into specific cable zones. You can buy one zone, multiple zones, or the whole system (which is also known as the interconnect.)

For your church, Cable usually is an ideal mass media solution, because the cable zone(s) may be a very close match to your Target Market Area/Footprint.

How do you buy cable? Not all channels are available for sale. Channels dedicated to the broadcast affiliates are not available except through those station's reps. Many lower volume channels are not available for insertion either because the cable system may not have the equipment to make every channel 'insertable.' That said, there are still plenty of popular channels to choose from.

Show your cable rep your Target Market Area/Footprint map. They can then show you their cable zone map and together you can pick the zones that have the best match, to give you the least waste.

Now, which programming to choose? If you've been doing your Media Survey, that will help guide you. The cable rep will also have a lot of info about the demographics of who watches each channel and show.

Also, like radio, you want to make a buy that reaches your cable audience at least 3-5 times per week (called frequency). Research shows that any less than

3 messages will never really work. Any more than 5 is o.k., but you reach a point of diminishing returns.

Like radio, you can make the 3-5 frequency work with any budget, but plan for at least a 4-week schedule to give it time to work.

>Very Small Budget: Buy 1 program or show (on one channel).

>Small Budget: Buy one daypart (on one channel). A daypart is a multi-hour block:
>>Early Morning (6–10 A.M.)
>>Daytime (10 A.M.–4 P.M.)
>>Early Fringe (4–7 P.M.)
>>Prime Access (7 P.M.–8 P.M.
>>Prime Time (8 P.M. – 11:00 P.M.
>>Late News (11:00-11:30)
>>Late Fringe (11:30-1:00 A.M.)
>>Overnight (Overnight–6 A.M.)
>>(Note that these are basic definitions for the Eastern Time Zone. All other markets typically shift Prime Time back by one hour, which affects other dayparts.)

>Bigger Budget: Buy multiple dayparts (on one channel).

>Even Bigger Budget: Buy multiple dayparts (on two channels).

>Then add channels to your buy as you increase your budget.

Your cable rep can help you with the calculations.

If you're only doing branding in your creative, without a Call-To-Action or offer, you probably won't get any immediate feedback on your advertising. It may be working and your attendance increasing, but without a specific CTA, it will be harder for you to gauge the results.

Broadcast Vs. Cable

If your house has cable, you don't want a separate system that gives you cable channels on one system, and the broadcast channels on another. To solve this, the cable company agrees to carry the broadcast signal and run it through your cable system. This is called retransmission or carriage. What's most important to understand is that the broadcast channels/network affiliates (ABC, CBS, NBC, FOX) cannot be purchased through your cable rep – only through the broadcast sales force. That also means that they can't be purchased by cable zone.

<u>What If There Are Two Overlapping Systems?</u>

In some markets, you have overlapping systems, typically where a fiber-optic company, like Verizon's FiOS, has laid their system on top of another. Usually, these systems don't have the same percentage of penetration (number of households served) as traditional cable, and their zones are much larger. Sometimes the systems can be purchased through your traditional cable rep, and sometimes there's a separate sales force.

BROADCAST RADIO

Radio can be a great media to use to promote your church.

It's a low-cost way to reach a large number of people. Why? Because it's a very cost-effective delivery system. The towers and other associated equipment to broadcast radio have been in place for almost 100 years. So, the radio infrastructure is already paid for, and the cost to deliver your advertising is minimal.

Radio production costs (the cost to produce your commercial) are also very low.

But does radio match your targeted footprint (farm market) without a lot of waste?

Here, we're not talking about the cost per spot, but rather the cost to reach a single person. In most media, this is translated to the cost to reach 1,000 people, or CPM/Cost-Per-Thousand for easier and more consistent math.

How can you get an idea of the station's coverage?

The station may be able to furnish you with their own map, or you can go to: http://radio-locator.com/cgi-bin/page?p=maps

Once you find your market, you'll see a listing of all the FCC radio stations and their formats.

If you click on the "i" button, you get a page with detailed information about the station.

Note the Effective Radiated Power, which tells you roughly the size of the station. The maximum watts for an FM station is 100,000 watts, with 50,000 watts being more typical in a metro area.

You'll also see a link to Area of Coverage View Coverage Map. Click on this link and you'll see the approximate coverage of the station.

Don't put a lot of emphasis on where the station says it's located, because the FCC could have dictated this, as licenses were being sold. Instead, focus on the 'Local' coverage map that's shown in red. Is there a little waste or a lot of waste for you?

Without getting into a lot of complicated media math, here's a simple way to judge waste. Is the station's LOCAL coverage twice as big as your Target Market Area/Footprint? Then you'll have 50% waste.

While this may seem like a lot, radio's low costs can help offset the waste.

EXAMPLE:
Station WXYZ
- Average Spot Cost: $25.00
- Average Reach: 1,000 (based on ADULTS 18+)
- Cost-Per-Thousand (CPM): $25 divided by 1 (,000) = $25
- Adjusted CPM, with 50% waste: $50

Radio stations like to show themselves in the best light, so they use whatever 'demo' or audience they reach the best. The simplest way to cut through all the hype is to always look at the same demo or audience: ADULTS 18+. This demo can be used almost universally across all media.

Don't get caught up if your best target audience is 35-64. You're just using ADULTS 18+ as a consistent measuring stick.

There are over 50 radio formats being broadcast in the United States today. And those formats change and evolve. Here are the primary formats, and under each are multiple sub-categories:
- News, talk, sports formats
- Country music formats
- Contemporary hit radio (CHR) music formats
- Adult contemporary music formats
- Rock and alternative music formats
- Urban music formats
- Jazz and Classical music formats
- Oldies, Adult Hits and Nostalgia music formats

- Spanish and Latin music formats
- World music formats
- Religious programming formats
- Public, Government, Community radio formats
- College, student formats
- Other formats (children's, ethnic, brokered)

By formats, we're talking about the type of music and programming that the station carries. This is typically self-defined by the station. Every radio station has its own personality, through the music it plays, its announcers and even its jingles. But most stations fall under specific radio format categories that are used to track audiences and attract advertisers.

If you're not sure about a format, just look up the format online for a description.

What type of format and station to pick? Start by doing a survey of what your first-time attendees listen to. You can do this easily with an email follow up, and an online survey instrument, like Google Survey or Survey Monkey. Note that you will get a few stray answers, like people saying they heard about you on TV when you've never advertised there. This is common.

At the end of the book, we've included a sample survey.

Usually, the results will guide you in the right direction. If you ask for their top three radio stations and you get a reasonable number of samples, you'll start to see a direction.

How much radio to buy? This doesn't have to be a complicated answer, but a lot of media terms can get thrown into the mix that makes it confusing.

Here's the bottom line: You want to make sure that you reach your radio listening audience at least 3-5 times per week (called frequency). Research shows that any less than 3 messages will never get through to today's busy listener. Any more than 5 is o.k., but you reach diminishing returns for anything above 5.

Here's how you can make the 3-5 frequency work for any budget, but plan for at least a 4-week schedule to give it time to work.

> Very Small Budget: Buy 1 program (on one station). A program would typically be a 1-2 hour block, with a particular host or content.
>
> Small Budget: Buy one daypart (on one station). A daypart is a multi-hour block:
> > Morning Drive Time (6–10 A.M.)
> > Midday (10 A.M.–3 P.M.)
> > Afternoon Drive (3–7 P.M.)
> > Evenings (7:00 P.M.–Midnight)
> > Overnight (Midnight–6 A.M.).
>
> Bigger Budget: Buy multiple dayparts (on one station).
>
> Even Bigger Budget: Buy multiple dayparts (on two stations).
>
> Then add stations to your buy as you increase your budget.

Your radio rep can help you with the calculations.

Remember that if you're only doing branding in your creative, without a Call-To-Action or offer, you won't get any immediate feedback on your advertising. It may be working and your attendance increasing, but without a specific CTA, it will be harder for you to judge the results.

Religious Stations?

Your first inclination may be to advertise on the religious stations in your market. Maybe that's what you listen to, or a lot of your congregation likes. Here's the challenge. Typically, the audience for those stations is made up of people who have a church home and are regular attendees or members. If you're going after the unchurched, or under-churched, there may better stations to use.

Two Coverage Maps

For AM Stations, there will usually be two coverage maps. One is for daytime, and the other for nighttime. Some stations were granted a license to broadcast at a higher power at night, and some stations don't broadcast at night at all.

Sixty-Second Or Thirty-Second Spots?

The radio industry is trying very hard to move from :60 spots to :30 spots because it's more profitable for them. The rule of thumb used to be that :30s were typically priced at 80% of the cost of :60s. While this does represent a cost saving, it's only a value if your message can be well executed in a :30. If not, then there's no value. In general, you want to look at :60 spots so that you have time to help 'paint the picture' for the listeners.

Satellite Vs. Terrestrial Radio

At the time we're writing this book, satellite radio has between 10% and 15% of the listening audience. Satellite radio would be Sirius/XM radio, that's obtained through a subscription. At this time, satellite radio is starting to become available on a local basis. (Terrestrial is the industry term for radio stations with traditional towers, etc.)

Internet Radio

When it comes to Internet radio, you have two main choices: a local station who also broadcasts their programming on the Internet, and streaming music services such as Pandora and Spotify. We are not big fans of paying for the local radio station's Internet audience. Why? Because you don't know where they live. They could be a former city resident that now lives in another state, who uses the station to stay connected. Or they live in Russia and just like the music the station plays. If the station offers it to you free, great. But our policy is to never pay for it.

Streaming services? Many are working toward the ability to offer local advertising. Will they be able to deliver ads as effectively as terrestrial radio remains to be seen, but it's worth keeping an eye on. The same basic rules of frequency apply.

OTHER MEDIA

Here's the best way to evaluate all other media, whether it's billboards, magazines or coffee shop flyers.

1. Analyze it. Look at the distribution of the media (where does the media primarily reach?) against your farm market and the map you created of your members and attendees. Does the footprint of the media match your church's footprint? You don't have to get overly analytical, but you can use your common sense. Does it seem like there's a lot of waste? If it seems like there's too much waste, then the results may prove to be less than you're expecting.

2. Test it. Don't make a long-term commitment but take a term that's long enough to reasonably gauge the results. Depending on the media, it's probably between 30 and 90 days. You may get some pushback from the media rep but just calmly explain that you have a systematic approach to advertising, and you want to make sure each of your advertising vehicles works like they should. If the rep really gives you a hard time or applies a lot of pressure that's not a good sign, so you should probably consider pushing back from the table.

3. Track it. As we've discussed earlier, track your results if possible, but realize that some media is difficult by its nature to track. Take billboards (outdoor) for example. Unless you're a convenience store that's offering a limited-time hot dog and soft drink combination, then your billboard advertising will be about branding and raising your church's awareness in the community. That's not a bad thing – but a good thing. It's difficult to track, so understand your goals going in.

OTHER OBSERVATIONS ABOUT ADVERTISING

K.I.S.S.

You've probably heard of this acronym – it's been around awhile.

K.I.S.S. is an acronym for "Keep It Simple, Stupid" or "Keep It Short And Simple" or just "Keep It Simple".

What you may not know is that it was developed by the U.S. Navy in the 1960s as a straightforward way to approach designs - that most systems work best if they are kept simple rather than made complicated; so simplicity should be a key goal in design and unnecessary complexity should be avoided.

There have been other similar phrases over time:
> Occam's Razor: The simplest solution is usually the best solution."
> Leonardo da Vinci: "Simplicity is the ultimate sophistication."
> Mies Van Der Rohe: "Less is more."
> Antoine de Saint Exupéry: "It seems that perfection is reached not when there is nothing left to add, but when there is nothing left to take away".

How does this apply to your marketing?

In two ways.

1. Give your advertising materials a K.I.S.S. test before they are finalized.

Are you communicating one single (and simple) thing in the piece? The more things you add over and above the primary communication message takes away from the primary message.

2. Do one thing well.

It's better to do one great mailer than try and do two average mailers. If you have limited resources (time, people and money) – and who doesn't, focus on fewer advertising projects rather than more. When you have the option to make the decision for more or less, choose less.

DO YOU HAVE A LEAKY BUCKET?

In 2005, Benchmark Portal (a contact center best practices organization) conducted studies to evaluate the state of email response by small to medium businesses in North America. As prospective buyers, they sent emails asking for information about high-value products and services through web forms or email addresses provided on the company websites. The companies were then evaluated on both their response time and the quality of the response (if any was received).

The results, while shocking, show the opportunity that's available to businesses who realize how to convert prospects that have been to their website.

> 51% of the companies did not respond at all
> 70% of the companies failed to respond within 24 hours
> 79% of the companies responded with inaccurate or incomplete answers

How does your church perform when it comes to website response? Do you have set standards for response, and do you monitor them regularly? Do you have a different response time for work hours vs. after hours? What about your response plan for phone calls and phone messages?

If you haven't addressed these issues, you may have what we like to call the "leaky bucket." Prospects are coming into the "bucket" but "leaks" in the bucket are causing you to lose some of them – leads that you worked hard to get in the door.

The good news? It's an easy cure. Step back and pretend you're a church prospect. Evaluate each step of the process. Then take the steps to make sure the prospect's communication expectations are met. Also, look at other churches systems, and those outside your business.

THINGS CHURCHES SHOULD QUIT.

Church Marketing Sucks (and Bob Goff) have run a couple of columns on what you should consider "quitting" as a church. We've culled out the ones that apply to advertising and marketing.

1. Quit sending crappy emails. Use a real email service. (Repeat after me: "BCC is not for me.") Pay attention to the stats. Craft your subject lines. Send content that's actually important. Learn how to do email marketing.
2. Quit doing stuff without a strategy. That feeling like you're not getting anywhere, like you have no traction? It's because you're just spinning your wheels. You have no strategy. Get one.
3. Quit treating your designer like a print shop. Respect their creativity, don't just boss them around. They are professionals, and you should learn how to work with them.
4. Quit treating the church database as an IT issue. It's an under-utilized resource. You should be integrating with it, finding ways to improve and protect it.
5. Quit ignoring typos. Seriously, buy a dictionary, get a proofreader, take a minute to read something before hitting print. The church has far too many typos, and it needs to stop.
6. Quit writing long web content. Nobody's going to read that much. Cut your web copy in half.
7. Quit assuming people will just show up. They won't. They've got better things to do on a Sunday morning. Communities are growing while churches are shrinking.
8. Quit giving events cool but useless names that don't describe the event. Elevate? Vertical? Collide?
9. Quit waiting for opportunities to just show up. You can't wait for them to knock on the door. You have to go get them.
10. Quit half-hearted start-ups on social media channels. It's good to reserve your name on up-and-coming social media channels, but your once a month post on Pinterest, Instagram or Twitter just doesn't matter. Give it up.
11. Quit using acronyms for ministry names.
12. Quit the multiple channels for individual ministries. Your church is spreading itself too thin. One Facebook page is enough.
13. Quit reacting. Start planning.

14. Quit Facebook. It may be strategic, but sometimes it's not fun anymore. For some people it's too much in-fighting. For others it's become "Bragbook." It taps into a dark place of failure by comparison.
15. Quit assuming the whole church needs to know about smaller ministry events. Specialized or targeted ministries shouldn't be splashed everywhere to reach a general audience.

PLANNING AN EVENT? DON'T FORGET TO USE YOUR MOST EFFECTIVE ADVERTISING METHOD.

If you're planning an outreach event, advertising it can sometimes be your biggest single cost. But many churches have found that the best (and cheapest) form of promotion is word-of-mouth. Start months in advance and equip your members with invite cards. Look at your other 'free' channels like your website, newsletter, social media and emails. Do a reminder and reprint and redistribute the cards a few weeks ahead of the event. You may still have to do some additional marketing, but at least you have a head start that cost very little.

NOTHING TRUMPS A STACKED OFFER.

Create what we call a stacked offer. This means adding multiple items to make the offer look so good that a good prospect is drawn to the offer. This tactic is used successfully in direct marketing, major retailers and by department stores. *Buy now and you'll get free shipping. Buy in the next hour and get a free carrying case. Mention this ad and you'll get a second item free. (All for one product!)*

A recent mailing from a car dealer had these offers:
    a. Payment Reduction (pay a lower monthly payment than you have now)
    b. 100% Trade Value
    c. Discount of $9,000 off MSRP
    d. Special Financing – 0% for 60 months
    e. Buy my vehicle back for cash
    f. $5 Cash Simply For Coming In!
    g. FREE Hot Dogs & Sodas!

Another offer was lease or buy any Volkswagen and get:
   a. FREE iPad Mini 2
   b. iWatch
   c. Apple TV
   d. Xbox One
   e. Beats Headphones

Think about it. This is how 'stacked' the car dealers made the offer, and for products that are sexy, fun, and tangible. We have to work even harder to sell people on your church. The dean of retail advertising, Claude Hopkins, sums Stacked Offers this way: *"The offer should be so attractive that only a lunatic would say no."*

How do you create a stacked offer? Think about your target prospect and then think what you have to offer on a regular basis:
- Outstanding kid's program!
- Nursery for babies and toddlers!
- FREE coffee!
- Come dressed as you are!
- FREE gift for visitors!
- We'll never do anything to embarrass you!
- Great music!

Then add anything else that you're doing promotionally:
- FREE Hot Dogs & Sodas!
- FREE Pizzas
- FREE flower for all mothers (Mother's Day)
- FREE U.S. Flag on holidays
- Bounce house for the kids.
- FREE drawings for XXX and ZZZ.
- Kids Facepainting
- Etc.

The more things you add, the more prospects you'll attract. These may seem cheesy or corny, but they work.

HAVE QUESTIONS? NEED MORE HELP?

I'm available to answer questions or give you some general directions, usually at no charge if the involvement is minimal.

You can reach me at:
    Brad Baker
    bradbaker@mac.com
    813-528-3291
    106 Gibbs Circle
    Beaufort, NC 28516

MEDIA SURVEY

Thank you for attending XXXXX XXXXXX church.

We'd like to learn more about how you heard about us, so that we can better reach more people, and would appreciate your help with this quick survey.

PLEASE NOTE THAT THIS SURVEY IS ANONYMOUS, WITH ALL ANSWERS KEPT IN STRICTEST CONFIDENCE.

1. How did you first hear about XXXXX XXXXXX church, and/or what prompted you to visit? (Only 1 answer please)
____ Internet
____ Relative
____ Friend
____ Neighbor
____ Co-worker
____ Direct Mailer
____ Radio
____ Television
____ Other: _____

2. What are your top 3 favorite radio stations:
_____ #1 station
_____ #2 station
_____ #3 station

3. What are your top 3 favorite television shows:
_____ #1 show
_____ #2 show
_____ #3 show

Is there anything else you'd like to tell us?

_____

_____

Thank you for your time. Your answers will help make XXXXX XXXXXX a better church!

MODEL RELEASE
XXXXXXX Church

In consideration of my engagement as a model, and for other good and valuable consideration herein acknowledged as received, upon the terms hereinafter stated, I hereby grant XXXXXXX, their legal representatives and assigns, and those acting with their authority and permission, the absolute and irrevocable right and permission to copyright and use, re-use and publish, and republish photographic portraits, pictures or video and film footage of me or in which I may be included, in whole or in part, or composite or distorted in character or form, without restriction as to changes or alterations, from time to time, in conjunction with my own or a fictitious name, or reproductions thereof in color or otherwise made through any media at their facilities or elsewhere for art, advertising, trade, or any other purpose whatsoever. I also consent to the use of any printed matter in conjunction therewith.

I hereby waive any right that I may have to inspect or approve the finished product or products or the advertising copy or printed matter that may be used in connection therewith or the use to which it may be applied.

No press releases, public statements or other media material concerning XXXXXXX or referring to XXXXXXX in any way shall be made by me or any person acting on my behalf without the express written approval of XXXXXXX. I may make favorable incidental reference to my association with XXXXXXX.

I covenant and agree that I will not at any time, whether during or subsequent to the term of this agreement, in any fashion, form or manner, unless specifically consented to in writing by XXXXXXX either directly or indirectly, use or divulge, in any manner whatsoever, any information of any kind, nature or description concerning the methods or procedures of conducting the business of XXXXXXX. I hereto agree that all such information is important, material and confidential and that said information critically affects the successful conduct of XXXXXXX business. I specifically agree that a breach of any of the provisions of this paragraph shall constitute a material breach of the agreement and shall mean that I shall be jointly and severally liable for any and all damages that result there from, including those damages that are consequential in nature.

I hereby release, discharge and agree to save harmless XXXXXXX, their legal representatives or assigns, and all persons acting under their permission or authority or those for whom they are acting, from any liability by virtue of any blurring, distortion, alteration, optical illusion, or use in composite form, whether intentional or otherwise, that may occur or be produced in the taking of said picture or in any subsequent processing thereof, as well as any publication thereof even though it may subject me to ridicule, scandal, reproach, scorn and indignity.

I hereby warrant that I am of full age* and have every right to contract in my own name in the above regard. I state further that I have read the above authorization, release and agreement, prior to its execution, and that I am fully familiar with the contents thereof.

Name:
_____
_____

Address:
_____
_____

City: _____ State: _____ Zip: _____

Phone Number: _____ SS Number: _____ _____ _____

Signed: _____ Date: _____

. . . .

Consent for Minors Only*
I am the parent and guardian of the minor named above and have the legal authority to execute the above release. I approve the foregoing and waive any

rights in the premises. *(Please write name, address and phone number on back if different than listed above)*

Signed: _____
Dated: _____

www.ingramcontent.com/pod-product-compliance
Lightning Source LLC
Chambersburg PA
CBHW050311220526
45465CB00005B/1942